Addicted to Sacrifice

(story of a codependent)

by Harris Guidroz Jr.

Introduction

Dark clouds, fear drips and evil overshadows. Dreams are replaced with resentment, passion - with anger. Love has been chained and locked away. I descend into a lifeless abyss. The smell of death envelopes my every pore. I bow before my tormentor, defeated.

Little did I know in a few months my life would change forever. I'd been beat down incessantly by multiple things in life, but I'd never been defeated. This time, however, I was. Stubbornness, nor pure will could help me overcome this demon. I had bowed to addiction. It had its hooks in me and to pull away or even try was excruciating. It would've been easier to pick up a gun than pick up the phone and ask for help. But, I didn't have a gun.

They sent me to rehab in Florida.

I'd been fighting life for a seemingly endless time, just wanting to die. However, there were a few times I was actually dying - and those were the times I didn't want to die. My liver stopped, my appendix ruptured, and I was in a fire explosion. Each was a near contract handshake with Death, but, I wanted to live. In the Florida heat, I thought over this, realizing I never wanted to die. All along, I just really wanted to *live*.

It was there I learned about codependency and that I'm an extremist. September, my recovery had begun; November, I was home and back in reality. I knew I'd need encouragement to not climb back down to where I was as well as overcome more.

November 9th, I decided to write a daily inspirational, detailing struggles and how to overcome them. To be sure I'd remain faithful to this commitment, I sent these to my friends around 7 every single day. I've not missed a day.

Being codependent is sacrificing your own desires and needs to make someone else happy instead - continuously. This forms an unhappy, resentful life. I know my codependent nature will always be there, but this journey helped me realize that my happiness is important too. I wrote these for me, but many people have texted me back and thanked me because it helped them. So of course, I'm trying to spread the help.

What it really was that changed and brought my life into something entirely new was my perception. I decided to really live instead of only survive. My environment didn't change, I did.

Smile; it's easy.

It is not how tall you are, it's how tall you stand.

I was thinking over childhood fears I had, like my fear of roller coasters. Even in mid life, those emotions felt current. It takes rational thinking of an adult to overcome those fears. What other fears, prejudices, and anxieties from then still clutch me today? There are traits, camouflaged, yet identifiable within us that have been modified because of our upbringing. There are parts of us that have been molded because of occurrences our subconscious couldn't let go of. In reminiscence, you can connect with those emotions. They feel real; they are real. There are parasites that cling to us into adulthood. We didn't shake them off before for not knowing how. As adults we either don't because we haven't identified them or because we have a block thinking "it's too late; I can't".

When we don't take care of what haunted us as children, they can magnify once in adulthood. It can be as simple as feelings of shame or guilt, or it can keep us in a feeling of disconnect, heighten entirety, and hold us in a dark pool of depression. A lot of anger can be released if we can just set free our childhood demons.

If an adult can handle the fears of a child, then why do we act like fearful children?

Part of the world's decline is the melting away of attention to anything or anyone. How often do you really engage with the people in your life? Gazes seem always averted, distracted. We're programmed to focus on work and self even if it means to break emotional ties - and then we're told that is good. We drive on our typical track week after week. We work and act like fleshly AI, going through the clockwork of what our inner gear says to do. We speak to each other, but run off the lines put in our head and react as is acceptable.

Life is too busy to stop. Is it really, though? We live in a selfish world. We all partake in selfishness like a bread we must feed on to make it. We do not realize it's that bread that makes us weak.

It is time to fight. Take a moment to stop. Just breathe; notice the air and what it contains. Turn your eyes to see the people around you. Notice them, speak with them, see them as more than just another part of your day. See the movement around you as life, life that hasn't happened yet and you're witnessing the birth of each new moment. Really see people, as experiences, emotions, ideas…as so much more than a body in passing. You'll be amazed at the difference it makes, and you may even begin to really care.

To bend to be socially acceptable is to sacrifice your will to be free.

Disappointment is an unfulfilled expectation. You have expectations because you have faith in something. In faith, you have hope. Hope, though, is like following the call of a siren. Relying on someone's else's action to receive your desire will likely end in disappointment. You have a better expectancy for something to be accomplished, though, if you are the one striving for it or at least part of the process. But, it feels easier to just have hope someone will aid your expectation.

Everything in life costs something. Are you willing to pay the price it takes to get what you want? In asking yourself this, sometimes your conclusion comes to that maybe what you want isn't as important as what you thought.

Excitement occurs when you see the beauty of something. However, you calm down when you find out the price. Can we decipher when it's wise to listen or to press on?

Most see a stop sign as an inconvenience, unless they're lost. The stop sign helps to notice your surroundings, notice there are more choices than just going straight. We remain mostly oblivious to the side roads until there is a stop sign. If you're lost, the stop helps you to get your bearings.

Life puts many stop signs in our path, although we struggle to look at them as opportunities. We want to just keep going straight; it's easier and faster. Changing direction can be scary because of its unfamiliarity. We keep traveling straight on, lost. We rather survive life than live it because it's familiar and what we've become comfortable with. If peace, love, and the truly joyous things of life are unfamiliar to you, maybe a change of direction would be good.

Do you belittle yourself because of yours or others' expectations? Are you your own worst critic? Does good or bad news travel faster?

People seem to hunger for bad news, especially gossip. Even good news can be carried on in a more judgmental light because it feels better off the tongue that way. Why? Think about the feeling of happiness that something good happened to someone else. The more distant the relationship, the more that feeling ebbs out. If there's no relationship, you may even begin to despise their good fortune. Think of how the people in your life respond to all the events in your life. If someone isn't actively helping or encouraging you to achieve your goals - they're not your friend. Don't worry about what they think because you don't even matter to them.

"A friend in need is a friend indeed." (Euripides 400 BC)

The way a codependent person behaves around you is how they identify with you. The less genuine they are, the stranger their behavior and the less they trust. Codependent people layer on a great amount of personalities as a shield and interchange between them as they see is best for the environment to survive. They act the way the person they're around wants them to act, to a degree, but in a stiff, distrusting way. They've been taken advantage of too many times to feel comfortable around people anymore.

Because of their multiple experiences, they have intense, almost clashing personalities. They become something from being treated a certain way for a long period of time. They can be the best friend you could never have imagined or a soulless nightmare that will drag you to hell if they have to go with you to do it. They are very patient, although when the patient runs out they can be a dancing flame of fury. They're very passionate and can care so much that if a leaf falls from a tree into their hand, they struggle to put it down. Yet, they could watch someone who they declared their enemy get hit by a bus without batting an eye. So yes, they'll go over the top to be whatever they decide to be to you or for you. They're the best at manipulation, you won't even realize they're doing it. Consider your options and deal kindly with a codependent person.

When your opponent can win by losing, you don't stand a chance.

I have more physical scars than anyone I know. Emotional scars, you just never know how many anyone has. By those scars we can be assured of our current strength. Most often, what we're currently going through isn't any worse than what we've been through. We can help ourselves be confident in knowing because we survived _____, then, this ain't sh*t.

Often, we lament what we think we've lost through our troubles or traumas, such as innocence. However, the fact that you maintained your integrity through that pain demonstrates you haven't lost anything. It's just that matured innocence, and other such things, looks so different, that it has usually changed its name by then. So, our virtues have not only grown, but we have also gained strength and other attributes we had yet to have.

Everyone has lost in life; it is how you move on that sets you apart.

There are three sides to every story - your side, their side, and what Truth has to say…

A man kills his wife. She was beating his child, so he struck her and broke her neck. It wasn't his intention to kill, but he did. We are judged by our actions and the result of them, not by our intentions.

If someone says something that strikes a chord wrong in your head, but you knew they didn't mean any hurt, you wouldn't be quite as offended. However, we only know what is spoken. So, your feelings are hurt and they don't even realize it. You believe they *should* know. Codependency. Instead of talking it over with the person, we just walk around wounded. We feel like we don't have a right to explain our feelings, but we have a right to be upset.

Pain can be avoided from just explaining how something makes you feel.

When you're going to a special meal, you starve yourself first. It makes the meal taste better. This scenario is true for every aspect of life. When you've earned something, you want it bad.

We've been programmed for instant gratification, which is no longer gratifying. People are unhappy because of it, not even realizing it's because they always get good things.

My climb out of the pit of despair was so extraordinary because I was so hungry to get out and wouldn't accept anything less. If you're not driven to chase after something in life you want, you're missing out on living.

Gratitude is the seasoning in life that makes everything better.

I was incredibly anxious about a package I had ordered. Almost every day, I would check the tracking; it never moved from the site of origination. Finally, May 9th 11:21 p.m., I got an alert. I was awakened by this notification. Was I happy to receive the good news at almost midnight? Nope!

We expect things to happen at a certain time in a certain way. We cause ourselves anxiety and frustrations thinking this way. We should just know that the end of bad or the beginning of good will eventually arrive, sometimes together.

Parts of our lives are predetermined by someone else. Not everyone can succeed in life; someone has to be at the bottom. What stops you from climbing, though? Many can identify what's stopping them, but won't go past knowing that much. Maybe knowing what's stopping them causes them to say, "Well, then I can't do it." The first step to making your own life and forging ahead is letting yourself know you can overcome the block.

I was at the very bottom, ready to die. I had a little left in me that decided to live. Every single day, that part of me pulled me through the battle. That part of me grew, refusing to believe I'd be anything less than what I wanted to be. I understood the difficulty of it, but I wanted to completely change my life and rise. I wasn't going to stop. Through that intense struggle came the birth of my greatest victory.

When I hear a voice say, "You can't do it." I know the voice is not my own.

What do you do for fun? Does it require being in a particular place? Does it take preparation for you to do it? The more qualification it takes for you to have fun, the more difficult it is for you to actually have fun.

Fun is something I choose, with or without activities I chose. I choose it for the everyday grind, which is as simple as putting your heart in it. I have fun at work, I have fun on my personal time, and wherever in between from one destination to another. Sure, I'd rather be at the beach, but I don't have to be to have fun. It takes being able to enjoy all the moments and the little things.

Wherever you are, if you have to be there - might as well have fun.

When I started going to the gym, I didn't notice the results for months. Other people noticed first. My goal wasn't to lift a certain amount, it was to show up every day. Achievement is made through daily consistency.

We want fairytale lives, or at least a pretty ending to each day. We want magic pills to make us thinner. We want quick ways to be rich. We put forth a lot of effort for our goals and get angry too quickly with ourselves because we didn't change. We throw in the towel then go curl up somewhere in a pool of inadequacy and dead desires.

Don't focus on the end result, for the length of getting there will slaughter your motivation. Reward yourself for being consistent. See one day as a victory, then work on the next. Give yourself acknowledgement for not quitting.

Being able to celebrate the small victories helps you make it to the end. The who you want to be is inside you.

I made a pledge to go to the gym every day for one year. After that year, I'd only missed 17 days of it. Afterward, I thought I'd go to the gym 3 times a week, now that my year's commitment was over. I failed, miserably. I got lazy and lost my initial spirit I'd started with. How do I reanimate that spirit?

It was in desperation that I found life to begin with. When you're at the bottom, the only way you can look is up. So, what do you do when you're in the middle and can go either way? It's easier to get from the bottom to the middle than the middle to the top. Like shedding 20 pounds, then trying to shed the last 10.

The only way I can see is to keep climbing. Make the middle the new bottom. I refuse to acknowledge there is a further down till I convince myself there isn't one. This way, I can only look up again and start to revive my spirit to climb.

When a baby is learning to walk, they struggle walking towards you. Once they get close, they fall into your arms. They give up the struggle once they see a safe place to rest. They don't yet realize that next is a thing called running. I've made it from the bottom of a pit, but now that I've made it to the top, I shouldn't just fall onto the ground and be done. I keep trying to move onward, as far away from the pit as I can.

Your good enough isn't your destination. Keep climbing.

A temporary change is useless. I transformed my life from what it was before. Very few make it from where I was to where I am. But, I have so much further I want to climb! I lived so much of my life never striving for personal achievement, because of ever feeding my codependency playing the supportive role for everyone else. When I let myself realize it's time for me, procrastination becomes the enemy.

My objective is to live life to its fullest starting with the plan to put it on paper. Don't aim for the temporary changes, they'll crumble and let you fall back to square one. Determine towards what you really want till you achieve it.

Your soul is you in your purest form. It's you when no one is watching, no self judgment, no restrictions. It's what you would do if there were no consequences.

Either you are an honest, decent person, or you appear to be. Whichever is true, eventually, people will realize it. Souls have a way of shining through. The only way to truly live is to be yourself. Perhaps the problem is not being able to admit to ourselves who we are, or we just care too much what others think. Until you get past that, you will never live.

Perhaps we want others to approve of us so much because it's even more difficult to get our own approval. To really be happy, you need to be able to express who you are. If you're constantly veiling yourself and trying to be what you're not, it just keeps piling up the stress. Lying is very stressful.

We are each other's audience, modifying our behaviors based on who's watching. We want to be accepted. We want to be able to make everyone happy. We become reliant on the adulation of who we are and how we are doing.

Why do we want to fit in so much? Maybe we have so much trouble finding comparable friends or companions because so many people are faking it. If you let your own colors bloom, perhaps it'll encourage someone else who is masking to be themselves too. The world gets so much more colorful when people stop trying to camouflage with everyone.

The one that hurts in the scenario of you putting on a sham is you. The only person who was to accept you is you. Show the world your soul and don't give a damn what they say.

Is there someone in your life that you're very comfortable with? I mean that person you call your best friend, not because they're around and they want that title, but you actually consider them that way. A lot of people have that one person that makes them feel valid and they can be who they really are when it's just them. They help you be brave. They show you that you do matter. Who you are around them is the real you, why not let them out always? Trapping that person is why your happiness gets trapped too.

The purpose of regret isn't to fix the past, it's to prevent it from happening again. It's a learning tool, not a pool to wallow in. If you just focus on your regret, you're going to make a lot more of it. Be mindful of your thoughts and actions. Choose a different path if you want a better future. Sometimes changing courses may start by looking at things in a different angle and working our way to doing better in big ways.

We work on the regret we later receive. Turn thirty, and you regret you didn't do more in your twenties. Maybe you have a weight goal within three months. At the end of those months, if you hadn't done it - three month regret. You didn't pick up your prescription the day before, regret the next morning. We need to be diligent to prevent regret. The present pain is worth the future reward.

A better life doesn't happen by itself, it's a result of hard work.

How would you describe a true friend? Some of the staple definitions would be someone who is there for you. They do their best to help you feel happy, and your happiness makes them happy. They'll sacrifice things for your sake. They're kind to you and will do things in your best interest. Sometimes, that same person can tell you truths that might hurt. They may tell you, perhaps, you haven't been yourself, that you have been letting things slip that shouldn't, that you've lost a light in your eyes and the desire to do things that shouldn't. It can really hurt when someone says things like that. Or they may become what seems pushy, but they're just trying to keep you from having excuses that are keeping you from succeeding. A friend is honest, even if it hurts.

Not everyone that heaps dung on you is your enemy, and not everyone that gets you out of shit is your friend. (Hindu philosophy)

An obsession is an idea or thought that insistently preoccupies a person's mind. A goal is the object of a person's effort, an aim, or a desired result. A goal is something real, something that we're actually moving towards. Obsessions are frustrating and time consuming without results. Obsession is liquid insanity running through your mind and can scare people away.

When you have a goal, it is ambition that moves you toward it. Lose your ambition and you lose your goal. Necessity is for drinking, breathing, and other such things that come naturally. Why don't we treat our goals as a necessity? Are you hungry to achieve them? When something is necessary to us, we get it done. We won't go a full 24 hours without eating or drinking, so why go a full 24 hours without working towards your goal at least a little?

Why don't we fight for life like we would for air?

A captive wishes for freedom. They may have a way to escape, but it would be painful, which dissuades them.

What are you in bondage to? Is the cost of freedom too high? We cage ourselves or hold still and let others do it. We have a way out, but we just won't let ourselves take back control. We act like we feel safer by giving others the control of our lives. Don't let others control your life. You're the one who put those people in control, you can take it back.

Trust is given to the faithful, but why do we so often give control to the selfish and unreliable?

We've all had our part in hell. Our view of past adversity determines whether or not the experience was wasted. The difference between the victorious and defeated is their outlook. *Look what I have overcome.* OR *Look how much I have suffered.* One's a victim, the other, a fighter. One wants sympathy, the other wants to help others, to encourage and inspire. It wasn't your choice to suffer, but it's your choice what you'll do with the knowledge of it.

Victories are won or lost by the attitude of the fallen.

We perceive that our sacrifice makes us good; without it, we are nothing. We put ourselves last, we jump to volunteer, we buy things others need…ever trying to be the one that makes the sacrifices. These things are all good, but do we ever stop to think that jumping to do something first keeps someone else from being the "hero"? If we're forever sacrificing, and refusing others their sacrifices to make, then aren't we doing an injustice within our charity? Sometimes always being the good guy becomes self insistence. Jumping in the way of others in the name of selflessness becomes selfish.

It is important for a giver to also receive.

People can have a tendency to instantly judge. After talking to someone for a few minutes, you may decide, *This person is so selfish*. You put that stamp of them in your mind, so every time you're around them, all you see is their actions as acts of selfishness. It's what you looked for, and that's what you saw. Even if they're not selfish, your mind looks for it, and then paints what they do in the light of it.

You may be self-loathing, so you can't help but see yourself as a failure. You've put that title on yourself, so when you really take a look at yourself, you see **Failure**. That's what you're looking for, so your mind brings up all the failure parts of your life and puts it on a big display when you self reflect.

A lot of the bad things we see do exist. Bad definitely exists. Good things exist too, though. If you look for good, you can find that as well as the bad.

Perhaps you have failed a lot and you continue to fail at some pretty big things or a lot of little things. Ever stop to think that maybe focusing on your failures is what has helped the continuation of failure? When we continue to focus on the negative, it keeps our emotions negative, which keeps our ability to properly function a bit off whack. Try to focus on things you've done well on, things you have accomplished, and things that make you happy. Thinking on the good things can help you to live better and think better till you begin to see that mountain of failure crumbling down.

If you start to look at others in a better lighting, then you will react to them differently. There may be a person you thought was a snob, but now you don't focus on that and you start to interact with them in a pleasing manner. It may take down their walls and they treat you better. Maybe they just acted snobby towards you because you were so stiff and judging around them before. Your actions impact how others react to you.

Remind yourself of positive attributes and you will be positive.

Ordinary is not given enough credit. My story has value because of where I came from and the intense climb to get where I am. I'm just an ordinary person. Looking at me and my life from the outside, I may seem like another average life. However, get to know me, my journey, and things I've been through, and the painting becomes so much more detailed.

We see ordinary things all the time, but where did those things come from? Thinking of where people and things came from, the lives, the stories - ordinary becomes so much more colorful and valuable.

If you can control yourself, you won't be so worried about trying to control the things in life you actually can't. What does it mean to control yourself?

Stay positive when everything seems negative. There's always an angle you can hold the broken glass that'll shed a beautiful spot of light across the wall. Staying positive will calm down a panicked room and help people to think more productively. There are many benefits to seeing things in a positive way.

When you feel like giving up, don't stop. You need to get past your "runner's high". Nothing like getting past it and that happy feeling washing over you that you didn't throw in the towel. Push yourself harder. Don't set yourself low goals. Aim high and really work to get there.

Always find a reason to keep going. When growing weary, it's easy to come up with a reason to stop. Refuse the invite to stop and "sit on the job", and outweigh those reasons with why you *will* keep going.

Fall in love with the idea of being that person every day. Don't say you want to be this person, but that you *are* this person, every day. If it's who you are, then, there's no stopping the train of success. Don't see it as a suggestion, but as your way of life.

The forest is always thickets at the tree line. Once you press in, you can see the journey is possible.

Helping a butterfly out of its chrysalis will prevent it from flying. It needs to struggle to free itself and prepare for flight.

We go out of our way to avoid struggle. We want things to be easy and we live in an age where things are made easier. Then, it isn't enough, and we want the difficulty level lowered - again.

Through adversity, the human spirit grows. Outstanding people with great accomplishments struggled to get there. Taking the easy road will keep you pretty mundane. A lot of people get comfortable with the simplicity of their unchanging lives. However, if you want to fly, you have to struggle. What do you want to achieve?

Some people really appreciate life. You see them and you think, *Wow, they really know how to enjoy life.* They didn't get there from going through the same cycle with no added struggle. They had to work to get there. You want to really *live*? You want to see just how much you can enjoy and love life? You need to be willing to struggle to get there.

The most crippling thing the world has done to this generation is make things easy for them. Who's going to hold their hand when an easy route isn't even possible?

If I beat you three times a day, but on Sunday, I only beat you once - you'll become grateful for Sunday. Being thankful for less unfairness still doesn't make the lesser of it any more right.

When you're codependent, you become everyone's trash can. We really want to help people, so we take in the things others really want to shed off and let go. When people see you as just the person that takes in all the negative emotions, all the bad stories, as well as all the nonsense others don't want to have to listen to, they won't come running to you with the good news. You're the garbage can; you're not made for something they want. They won't give you the things they want so you'll maintain your status. They need a garbage can; everyone does.

Does this mean you should stop trying to help people and solve problems? No. But people came to see you in this way by the way you show you see your own value. When you're willing to bow and be trampled to lift someone up, day after day, people will see your value as nothing more than something to get dirty and crushed. Learn how to help them throw away their trash without being the thing that swallows it.

The balance is don't think too highly of yourself while not letting anyone treat you low.

Intelligent people can do really stupid things. You don't ensure due diligence to be sure the decision was the best. You throw caution to the wind and just do it. You didn't really care about the outcome at the moment, or you didn't really consider the end results at all. You took the lazy way out.

One of the reasons you may take the lazy way out is from just being plain burnt out. The people around you have a lack of appreciation for what you do day after day. One day, you finally give up on your careful planning, and just make a quick choice. Everyone notices. Humans are rather prone to notice the negative more than the positive. There may be someone else who makes dumb choices all the time, blunders constantly, and isn't consistent with pretty much anything. People will quit noticing the bad they do, because it's done all the time. When people notice the times you mess up, you can comfort yourself in using this to realize that means they at least silently notice the good that's being done and subconsciously appreciate it.

Don't wait for others to verbally show appreciation, learn to appreciate yourself and just know you're making a difference.

Have you ever wanted to go somewhere, and the GPS seems to be pointing you in a completely different direction? You're heading to a destination that is east, but the GPS shows you're going due south. You focus on your GPS and the base ways you are going, not noticing anything but - Why the heck are we going south??

We can't become so focused on a goal, we forget to live and enjoy the days that take us there. Life isn't just about each goal we make it to, it's about the journeys we make. Yes, let's get there, but let's enjoy the moments, notice the little things, and really live life along the way. We don't have to wait until we achieve our goals to keep living. Living is the main goal, after all.

What is courage? A lot of people may say that doing some big heroic act or facing your enemies is courageous. It's sort of like success, though. Being successful doesn't mean you have a big house, lots of land, and a fat bank account. You can have the success in having and keeping a job, or success in keeping the weight off. Success can come in small or large doses, and whoever accomplished that should know it has value.

We try to have successful days or at least successful moments each day. We definitely need courage for our every day. When you face and overcome something big, you may realize that yes, you were brave. Because of the larger moments, we often fail to see how brave we are every day. It takes courage just to get out of bed. We underestimate ourselves when we don't realize all of our "little" victories.

The most courageous thing you can do is face every day with a smile.

We all hope certain things will happen. Do you have a lazy hope, not putting in any effort and just waiting to see if it will happen? Do you gamble your emotions on what you hope for? People expect too much, making their happiness hold their breath as they wait. Nothing is wrong in wanting things, but basing your mood and quality of life on it is definitely self depreciating. You can't bank your happiness in a future hope, it's not steady, at all. It's asking to be disappointed.

Too many people are stuck and waiting. "I'd be so happy if…" They refuse to believe that it's not because of a lack of things or events that's keeping them unhappy. If you're unable to make the choice to be happy now, you won't be able to make that choice in the future.

People say that they hate change. It isn't the change, but the disruption of the normal order, that we hate. We all get stuck in cycles, becoming comfortable in them because we know all the how, when, and wheres. Even if the routine generally makes you unhappy, or it's an unhealthy way of life dragging us down, it's what we stick with. It's what we know.

You get home, knowing the typical things you do once you get home. Your spouse, however, randomly brings up really wanting to go to the park. Initially, this strikes a chord of agitation and some discomfort. It wasn't what you expected. You become suddenly raked with disruption. When you get to the park, though, you really enjoy yourself and have a good remainder of your day. If you'd have had the foresight to know how it would've gone at the park, likely you wouldn't have been irritated at the change.

Being told, as a child, you were going somewhere and you didn't expect it - it's usually very exciting. The child knew what their day was going to be like, but when they get told, "We're going to the park." it's an immediate feeling of excitement. As adults, though, we've lost the amazement and wonder. Everything is affected by your attitude to the day. If you keep a positive outlook on the surprise twists, you can face each day with the excitement of a child.

The excitement of the young mesmerizes the old, because it's a gift they have lost.

Those who tend to hate most things also have a lot of pent up anger. Anger is like the pressure of a volcano. Each thing adds pressure; they use hatred as a way to vent. They may find they enjoy being hateful, feeling like it's an outlet for their frustrations. Hatred, however, doesn't solve anything.

You do not hate everything, you just don't know how to deal with the pent up anger. Perhaps you don't know where all that anger came from, or how to get rid of it. Once you identify where it's from, you can better deal with it. Being hateful only throws the boomerang of anger around. Dissolve the hatred instead of playing with it.

Why am I trying to walk on eggshells? People shaming others to believe in their "holiness" of opinions. If you have the freedom to believe your ideas, why can't I have that freedom too? You aren't special or chosen - get over it.

The pleasers are the ones tip toeing about, trying not to offend, trying to please and serve. We go too far till who we are drowns in the desires of others. You know your identity, but then you wrap in a cloak of what others want to see. Do you suppress who you are for others or for your own self shame? Self shame often comes because of the opinions of others. But - you have a right to be you as much as anybody.

Quit worrying about the shame others throw at you and you'll quit shaming yourself.

I was playing a game. I eventually noticed winning was merely based on what better or worse selection the computer laid out. It had little to do with the skill of the player. Do we have to play with the cards we're given? Can we take from the other options Life holds?

Part of being a decent human is following the rules of life. Rules are mostly not exclusive and others have to play by those same rules. Life is more about who you choose to be, the cards you choose to take up and toss away. You can choose to play smart or not think things through, or maybe just not care. Choose to play wisely and well. Stand up to your bullies, kiss the girl, take that chance, fall on your face and laugh at yourself, aim for your goals and achieve.

If bees don't have to be told it's possible to fly, then why can't you just know rising is possible for you?

Life will give you many chances on things. The chances of an intimate friend, though, will not pass you many times in life, if ever more than once. How many people have lost that chance because of how they lived their life with them?

A true friend finds value in you as well as in the moments they give you. They help you heal and they love you with your scars. You don't have to fear sharing your secrets with them. They like you as much as they love you. They don't hesitate when you're in need. They take up for you even when you're not around to see it.

How do people lose a friend so diligent to be there for them? Eventually, they will see you don't see or appreciate their value. They will see if you don't stand for them, when kindness is a one way street. Even with low self esteem, they eventually can see they're worth at least more than what you offer. Don't feel the regret of not treating someone right when it's too late.

You always have reasons why you treat them a certain way. You comfort yourself in saying why and what you do is legitimate. You know you can get by or away with something and keep receiving. You half ass things, and just get real good at words to cover your act up.

Is the relationship actually important to you if you treat it poorly? You may have convinced yourself that it is, but you've gotten to fooling yourself as well. If you don't take care of something, then, is it really important to you?

If you want to have a friend, you need to be one in return.

How do you respond to someone interacting with you? How we respond to others in the world says a lot about who we are. Do you feel like you haven't the time to be nice to everyone? Then that's a pretty good description of who you are. Are you rushing past people to make it to the top? Do you let go of relationships because of a lack of time? You're making great strides to make it to your goals, kicking up dust in the eyes behind you. Your responses are shallow, generic so you don't have to stop and fully listen.

What's the point of winning the race if no one is there to congratulate you at the end?

I asked a coworker if he knew how to balance an egg on its edge without support. He gave it a few awkward tries till I asked him if he wanted me to show him. I took the egg and dented one side so it could stand up just fine.

We all have questions - how do I make more money, why ain't I happy, how do I quit smoking, why can't I lose weight….Acting like the answer is a great mystery. We keep looking at the question and trying to answer it from one angle, from our first thought of how to do it. It's almost like we want to stay frustrated and let people see that. We try, we fail, we either quit or make another feeble attempt from the same thought process.

A lot of solutions are simple, but we're too busy trying to work it out in the most grandiose way to see the real answer.

I told a young man, if I could give you all the lessons I've learned through all the pain and stupidity I've endured and displayed, he would be highly successful. However, the only way for you to learn is for you to have the suffering yourself.

Often, we want to just keep looking forward and say that next time, you'll make the right choices. If we can't learn from our mistakes, though, how will we avoid future mistakes? We can have a new beginning by realizing we were wrong and then change course from where we were. We need a different starting point. Before you can get better, you have to be better.

Do you know people who get themselves to "fall in love" because they saw someone was lonely or needed a friend? They had pity, so they became that person's lover. Or someone who agrees to do something solely for the reason they were afraid of what they'd think if they told them no. Maybe someone wants to lose weight so others will see them as pretty.

If your ambitions are for the wrong reasons, you'll fail and even could hurt others. Don't do things to impress others, do it for yourself. Approach ideas and goals from the right angle. You can't control the opinions of others, so go with your opinion. Why do we let ourselves imagine our opinion isn't as validated or has as much worth as others? Be proud of who you are, and don't let anyone take that from you.

I love the rain. It's awe inspiring and beautiful. It can also be cold and may come with lightning, but I gladly welcome it all. Rain is necessary for life and growth.

Much like the rain, love is necessary to live. Wherever love in your life comes from whether friends, family, or your romantic partner, you crave it like water. A year ago, I realized all my life I'd been surviving a dry existence. Surviving, getting the bare minimum…then, I became determined to live. I wanted to experience all the aspects of love - the warmth, the beauty, even the cold of it, the painful sides. Love comes with its price, but its price is worth the bravery to keep it.

I've been trying a dating site for two weeks, and I've been through seven scammers. People trying to take advantage of someone looking for love or friendship. Why do people take advantage of and even abuse each others' friendships? Has someone ever taken advantage of your love? Used your friendship just when they needed it? Think of those times, then think of the times someone has really loved you. Even though those others used you seemingly endlessly, you never really were enough to them. You were never good enough and they let you know that until they needed you - then - for the moment, you were all they needed. There was no forgiveness in your relationship with them, no relent. Where there is no love, there is judgement.

People try to look for their match. They look for people with similar interests, someone they click with. It's almost too easy, though, to come across a match. Similar interests and the ability to smoothly have a few conversations isn't a true fit. There may be two puzzle pieces that look just like the other, but they may not fit each other at all. "Matches" will burn and fizzle out, but when you find your true fit, they're by your side forever. The path to finding your soul's flame is lined with hundreds of mimics.

When I am at the gym and I see a paper towel on the ground, I pick it up. It's not mine, and no one would think anything of me walking by, but I do it for me. I've lost too much to laziness, so I continue to work to stay away from it. I see forms of sloppiness, which reminds me of what laziness can look like. In return, it reminds me why I want to stay away.

Once laziness comes into one part of your life - not doing the laundry, the dishes, or cleaning spills, etc. - it will spread into other parts. You'll become lazy about relationships, your job, even the hobbies that make you happy. Laziness is like a poison; it doesn't take a lot to do harm.

Hitting the snooze button quickly becomes a habit. From there, it's struggling not to fall into other bad habits. Can I skip out on the gym today? It's just one piece of cake. …all because I hit the snooze button. Our criminal delusion is that we have more time and putting things off is a reward. You can always find an excuse not to do something. You're not rewarding yourself, you're excusing yourself.

Excuses are like weeds, if you don't pluck them out, they will continue to produce.

I need structure, or I become flustered. This week, my schedule had to be necessarily, but not regrettably, altered. The next week, I reverted back to my old schedule. I didn't regret the change the week before, and it all worked out well.

People become flustered from different things. The problem is, we use simple frustrations as an excuse to become angry. Things pass much quicker than we put on to ourselves. I could've let myself become quite upset about the differences going on the week before, but I kept my peace. Even in bad circumstances, we can thrive. Adaptability is being able to thrive with the resources we already have.

Why do so many people believe being rich and beautiful would make them happy? People blessed with those things kill themselves all the time. They obviously weren't happy, and it's not that they didn't know they were beautiful or know what to do with the riches.

Do you think you'd be a different person if you were rich? You'd still be you. Are you not happy now? Wealth won't do it for you. Happiness is waiting for you to reach out and pick it up. It's not in the next big job opportunity, or in that nose job you're hoping to soon afford - it's standing there, wondering why you haven't paid it any mind. Anyone has the ability to feel happy, but many have this reason they haven't reached over for it. Too busy, maybe, or too much on their mind…Who are you really? The you that you wish could be let out, but you're not willing to do the work to do it? Behave the way you would if you were who you wanted to be.

Things look very different when it's broken. What do people look like after being hurt countless times? The smart end up alone, unable to trust. The pretty become a shell, seeing only their reflection getting old. The kind become resentful…From there they believe, *this is the way things are*. Do you realize after you've left those who have broken you, if you let yourself remain what it turned you into - you're still being their puppet? Define who you are and let the broken shell shed off. You don't have to be what they left you to be.

There was a child in a poverty stricken area. A missionary wanted to buy him a Haagen Dazs ice cream. The boy replied that that would be cruel because it'd be the only one he'd ever get. At first thought, he may have seemed like a very wise young man. However, think about it…

That boy may very likely still be poor today. He was never able to have that ice cream he turned down because of his dejected attitude - the attitude that - *it's never my turn*. With this outlook, when your turn does arrive, you won't take it.

You'll never have victory in your life if you live in a defeated mindset.

I have a friend that loves animals more than people. If she had to choose between saving an animal that she'd seen for the first time and me - I'd know, *I'm gonna die...*

Animals are intensely forgiving. They don't take things personally and see your anger as a cycle. They go to their little spot and take a nap while you do your thing. Humans are definitely not so forgiving. They take things personally, most often, too personally. They see others' emotions as always directed at them, take conversations in the way their mind may twist them, and see gazes as meanings they invented.

Humans fight back and see it as they have a right to. In confusion to the sudden aggression, the first will fight in return - all because of assumptions. Humans are the only creatures who use assumptions like we do.

Think twice before acting on your first assumption. See others as if looking from the inside and be them for a moment. Know there is something more and nothing may be directed at you but perhaps their phase they're going through...you'll understand kindness and forgiveness on a whole new level.

It can take being blind to ourselves before we can see anything else. It's a natural tendency to think of ourselves, which is alright, but not in the way we often do. It's as though we want to infect people with the knowledge of us. When others are speaking to us, we're not listening, we're thinking - thinking of what we'll say next. We distribute knowledge like seeds, hoping they'll grow. We want others to really realize what we see, think, and feel. We detrimentally want to make ourselves relevant to the world around us.

Ever think about everyone else around you feeling the same way? Who's going to stop and listen? Who's really going to be remembered? Having a good self-esteem is to want to help others instead of having to make yourself relevant to them. When your heart is healthy, you affect the world instead of infecting it.

Your behavior is part of your routine. You expect more bad from life, but are seldom surprised by anything good. Your expectancy for the bad mellows out the good. You half heartedly go through your daily motions because you expect nothing more than *having* to live. Their argument is that you shouldn't have high expectations because of disappointment. Living in a constant dull, however, is no better!

Expect good from your day and from yourself. Set goals and achieve. I don't set in my mind that I have to win; I set in my heart to never stop trying.

Children are afraid of the dark. As adults we realize it's an unrealistic psychological fear. The dark has no substance that can actually hurt you. …we as adults are afraid of other people's opinions. These, likewise, have no substance that can actually physically do us harm. We worry insistently about others' opinions more than our own. Smile and live while others shake their heads. Show your opinions matter to you and what you do.

I do care and I don't want to hurt anyone or their feelings. I also want to live my life. If I'm decadent and honest and also want to stand with my opinions and dance - what is it to anyone?

Trade your shame for happiness.

It makes me angry when people manipulate me to get their way. When something doesn't work, they try from a different angle. When they're honest and it doesn't work, they just get pissed off.

Solution: Knowing what you want and expressing it is important, but getting it is not always your choice. You have to be OK with that.

It seems people aren't friendly anymore, or such a person is now scarce. There are nice people, willing to hold a door, or say a quick hi, or *I like your outfit*, but ultimately, people are reclusive from true contact. Always on their phones, they only interact when necessary. It's true if you want to have friends, then be friendly, but people are afraid. They're afraid to take chances. What's especially sad is when someone tries to be friendly, but others are so distrusting, they block it immediately. So, we end up with a selfish and lonely society.

If we made it a goal to try to be friendly as often as we checked our social media, the world would not be dying.

I used to imagine that every leaf on a tree had a wish. If someone caught them as they fell, their wish would come true. Have you ever fallen? Did you catch yourself before you hit the bottom? Perhaps there was a friend or a higher power that caught you.

Every time I've ever fallen, I was caught before I hit the ground and vanished into oblivion. Looking back, I am strengthened to know that no matter where I fall from, I have a net. I'll be able to go through whatever I face. Often, amiss all our adversity, we forget what we've already overcome. When we remember our victories, that's when we find the strength to continue to fight.

No strings attached. Why is that phrase so alluring? It's fun without responsibility. Every person, pet, or object you have a relationship with or own has a string attached. We chose to have those strings. If something meant enough to us or we wanted it badly enough, we were willing to take on those strings. We knew the price and we were willing to pay. The question is, are you tied to this string, or is it tying you down? If you buy a car, it helps you get where you need to, but if the payments are too much for your income - it's tying you down. If you have a dog that gives you company, but he won't stop tearing things up and you spend more time angry at it than happy with it - it's tying you down.

If I'm being pulled off a cliff because of something I'm tied to, I'm going to cut the string.

When we have hatred for someone or are angry about something, how much does it really affect that other thing? If I'm cursing out a bad driver, are they even really going to know? Then I go on for ten minutes, angrily thinking about the moron, whilst they are just going about their day, never aware of me. How much of our lives are wasted on harmful emotions? Hatred is a poison you keep inside, harming yourself and possibly never even reaching what it's meant for.

There's a child on an Easter Egg hunt. He knows in one of the eggs,there's a five dollar bill. He wants it badly. The adults turn all the kids loose. He grabs egg after egg, but never finds the big purple egg that holds the five dollars. Devastated, he rides home without looking in his bag. Once he gets home, he goes through them and realizes he had six one dollar bills. All along, he could have enjoyed the little things, but he was too busy thinking about what he'd originally hoped for.

Waiting on the one big thing that never comes. You fail the little moments, glorifying how your big day will be. You could've enjoyed all the happiness along the way, but couldn't see them with your eye forever on the spyglass. It's not until you look back and take an inventory you realize how really blessed you are.

Enjoy your little moments before they're packed away as only memories.

Monday was rough. I said if I woke up and it was Monday again, I would stay home.

Ever get a notion about a day before it ever gets here? Have you thought poorly of a day, and then, it went all to pieces - *just like I said it would*. I wonder how many bad days you've had because that's the way you approached it.

There are problems you've faced and you just felt empowered with your *I got this*. You fixed it, conquered it, and maybe even gave someone a grinning *I told you so*.

Our attitude composes the majority of our lives. We write our own stories with the pen of that attitude. I've alleviated the majority of my anxiety simply by telling the truth and doing my best every day. When I mess up, I own it and fix it. It can be a hard thing to do, but being a frightful, lazy liar is much more painful. Usually the problem isn't that you're not good enough, it's that you're not trying your best.

Tomorrow will bring trials, but - I got this.

I was talking to a friend's wife who has a toddler. She was complaining about having to be the "bad guy", whilst her husband came home from work and was the "fun one". But, who does the child run to when hurt, sad, or afraid? They run to the one who nurtures them the most, who picks them up when they fall all through the day, who corrects them when they're wrong…they run to the one they *know* can fix the problem.

You're an adult now. When you have problems, which direction do you run? It seems like the world's common habit is to run towards fun. Drink away or smoke away your problems, or maybe you have a quick fling to help you forget. We want to escape problems by postponing the inevitable conflict. Sometimes a child in its simplicity has a greater grasp on reality than adults.

There's a child in you, running scared, looking to you to be the adult now. That child needs to be comforted knowing there's an adult in charge. When you act responsibly, the child in you feels safe.

The snooze button is one of the declines of western civilization. You can tell when you're slacking off when you're hitting the snooze button, whether literally or metaphorically. Finding motivation is an incredibly elusive quest. *How do I become motivated?* My best answer so far is through discipline. Build it the same way you'd build muscle through exercise. Pick something you can be disciplined at and will do consistently every time. For me, it's cleaning my kitchen before I go to bed. Once you prove to yourself you can be disciplined in one area, you can work on another till it expands through your life. Do it for yourself and enhance your life.

Discipline is learned through practice and patience.

Clouds are fun to look at. I love them when they're white and fluffy or dark and brooding. Sometimes, though, when it's especially bad, it's so dark and muddled, you can't tell one cloud from another or really tell the sun exists anymore. All you know or at least can really think about is the awful storm.

When you're in a dark place in life and can't see any light, you sometimes choose to embrace the darkness because it has become all you know. It's not until you choose to be happy that you can see there's a better place to be. Just because the good, happy, and bright cannot be seen doesn't mean it doesn't exist - it's just out of sight.

What robs your willpower to be better? Why do you accept a lesser version of yourself? You could realize what you're capable of if you just apply yourself. Or, even, you know what you're capable of, but you won't take the steps to get there. There's work involved and a lot of hard kicks along the way. It's the awareness of those kicks that robs us of our will to continue.

We have full control of a limited part of our lives. There are the terms and conditions that we've accepted along the way that control us: work, pets, spouse, children, payments, etc. Even though these are, or can be, good things, they take away control and time from our lives. How do you take a step up for you? Where's the control to be that better you? When do you wake up? Is it right before things have to get done, or do you actually give yourself some time first? How much time do you waste doing nothing in your free time? Start with these things. Intensify your focus and motivation in the simple places where you know you have control. From there you can build and amaze yourself.

The things that take control don't wake up at 4 a.m., that's why you should.

What do you think of when I say *Spam*? …Unsolicited, unwanted… Have you ever considered that some of your actions may be spam?

A codependent person doesn't want to see people struggle, at all. But…struggle is what life is about, or at least composed of. You have to go through it in order to grow. Often, our help is unneeded, but we like to keep popping up anyway. People need to figure things out for themselves. Problem-solving is a developed skill. When someone is going through something difficult, they need to heal through realization and struggle. They may need *some* help and empathy, but not a full "I'll carry you" above all their sorrows. Consequences are for intellectual development, keeping similar mistakes from happening. You put your hand in fire once, you won't do it again.

Codependents want to go overboard with help till they even do things they just really shouldn't. So, when you offer to take action or do a good deed, ask yourself - Who am I helping and why? What will be the outcome, short and long term, if I help? Is my help really needed or wanted?

Sometimes being nice makes a bad situation worse.

Years ago, our cat caught a rat and I was charged with dispatching it. I ended up not having the heart to kill it, so I let it go on the edge of our property. When I came back to the house, my wife asked, "Did you take care of it?" I said yeah, I "took care" of it.

Our perception goes hand-in-hand with our emotional state, picking to believe the things that validates its thinking. If you're happy, things are positive. If you're sad, things are negative. If you're paranoid, the worst is going to happen. Within multiple possibilities, your brain picks one and believes it. Judging a situation, unbiased, is seldom done and not easy. Although the other person may not think the same as you, that's how they feel and it's real to them.

The multiverse is a real thing; it's inside our heads. We alter the true universe every day.

You may have figured it out, but I believe in God. So yes, I do pray.

Do you know what your hopes and goals are? What are you praying for?

When you don't have to do the work to get something you want, you're jumping right into it. When you realize the height of the work, you set your sights a lot lower. It's not that you can't achieve the top, it's that you don't want to work for it.

No matter what path you choose, there will be hardship. So, you need to pick a life that's worth it. Only praying and sitting won't get you through anything but being dragged through the bottom rungs. After you pray, you still have to stand.

Today was the first time I saw my neighbor appear in the window of the condominium complex 75 yards across from me. I could see him clear as day, which was a humorous thing to realize…having a room with five windows, which I clean wearing nothing at all.

If we could see a clear view of ourselves, would we behave differently? *Do* you see yourself? How do other people see you? What do they say of you? Even if they've only seen some of you, what do they see? People believe that you are the way they see you.

When we're gone, the one thing we leave behind are the memories of us.

A belief will not change you or your behavior, but a conviction will. There are many things we are aware we believe, but we also ignore. Just think of the things people are aware are bad for them, but still do them.

In today's landscape, a person with a conviction is considered radical. Honestly, many are. However, the fear of being pinned as something bad is what "copy, paste"s a general population. Self expression and individual identity is trying to be held back. People identify with the general population to be like everyone else. Even some of the categories people can be part of that's considered "different" and/or "set apart", they're just another generalized group that was concocted. If we allow ourselves to melt into the identity that was chosen for us, we'll lose our individuality.

What is your identity? Block out the static of the world, find yourself, and be the best version of you. And, do it for you.

The morning started with an amazing sunrise; I had to stop and take notice.

Did the day go the way I wanted it to? No, nor did I get the end result I was hoping for. The day was challenging and exhausting, but I did my best. Our day should give us a feeling of accomplishment, not necessarily because things happened just right, but because we gave it our all. We make each day impossible for us to win because of our predeterminations.

I didn't tell myself I'd get what I wanted. I just did all I could. Because of this, my day ended as beautifully as it began.

Passion can be a great and helpful tool. However, its unstable power makes it difficult to channel it correctly. You're much more likely to be irrational in a moment of passion, leaving at least some destruction in the rear view.

If you're a vindictive person, you revel in the suffering of someone else. Another may suffer from gossip you may spread, isolation from your care, tearing down their character, etc. What do you participate in that deteriorates and tortures others? Suffering is torture to the one within it. For a major example, what of the Nazis who tortured the Jews? How do you judge them? What about someone who beats their spouse? Do you judge them? How do you vindicate what you do?

If you're honest with yourself about your actions, you may realize you're enacting malice, not justice.

Ever put furniture together? You try to follow the directions so you can enjoy your end product. Are there directions on how to put life together? Sadly, life isn't as simple as even the most complex furniture pieces. We can, however, construct our lives.

Are you trying to put your life together, but keep coming up to the same frustrations? You keep trying the same way, effort after effort. You learned some from those you grew up around and your own knowledge you gleaned along the way. Now you have all these pieces and it's time to build your own adult life.

To keep trying is admirable. Stopping to reevaluate is important too, though. Perhaps it's your lack of contentment as you aspire for a higher life. You think your happiness is only ahead. In frustration, you keep trying to cram the wrong screws in and put the leg where the arm of the chair is supposed to be.

Life is beautiful. You have to appreciate the one you have for the peace to climb higher.

You can "change" for a day, but to really be a better person - you have to evolve into it. A person may leave an abusive relationship, but then end up in another one. It's not just that they abuse you, it's that you let them. They forever resent that person because they never wanted to give themselves in that way.

Codependency is my behavioral tendency; I'll always have it. I did let myself recognize this behavior and over time learned to control it and channel it in the way I wanted it. I'm still a giving and self-sacrificing person, but I now just do it when I want to.

The giver that gives what he doesn't want to is resentful, contemplating all his losses.

People can subconsciously isolate themselves to varying degrees, depending on their environment as a child. If you had to process your own emotions and situations, you felt ultimately alone. This form of self preservation is based on perception, not reality. It's selfish to believe no one cares about you. You'd be surprised how many would come to your rescue if needed. The problem is, you don't exhibit the need for it. You can't expect people to notice the little hints you leave and understand your needs.

People need to show love, but don't always know who to give to. Don't be afraid of rejection; give others a chance and place to send their love.

It takes a lot of effort, time, and money to keep up our outward appearance, to be the most beautiful us we can. People stress about diet, clothing, skin care, exercise…but not always for health reasons, it's to "be attractive". What about putting as much effort into our character traits as we do with our outward body?

Are you trying to hide what's underneath? Why not make it where you don't have to?

Sometimes it feels like I wake up and five years have flitted by. All the things I could've or should've done are still on that "soon" shelf. I'm only older in the same place.

It's said the way to eat an elephant is one bite at a time. Your ambition may have fizzled because you tried to bite too much by setting your first goal too high. Then, when you can't accomplish that monumental task, you give up.

Life isn't a contest, it's a trial. How long have you already waited? Are you just waiting for the "magic to happen", or are you taking the bites? It's not the size of the goal, it's the consistency you apply when conquering it.

Doing a little is better than wanting to do something great and doing nothing.

The power of words is through listening. If no one listens to what you say, then your words are meaningless. Being a good listener is just as important as being a good orator. If two people are speaking, but neither is listening to the other, they might as well go talk to themselves.

You only have a right to voice your opinion when you've really listened. If your goal is to only win the argument, you're stagnantly hearing only your thoughts while the other is trying to voice theirs. If you both speak and pay attention, your goal is a resolution - not just to be right. Then, others will stand with you.

Listening shows you care. Even if you disagree in the end, the unity can remain because they feel you still truly care - not about the topic, but them.

Words are like toothpaste, once they're spoken, you can't put them back. If you call someone stupid or ugly, they'll always remember that you said that. Even if you try to tell them otherwise, they'll probably forever see the first words as the truth.

What about when you do the opposite? You tell someone they're brilliant, that they're funny or a great friend - they'll remember those words long after you say them.

I never use flattery. If I compliment someone, I mean it and they have earned it. People typically learn over time who is the flatterer and whose compliments have weight.

Has anyone ever told you something that really brightened your day? Do you later remember it and it helps you through the moment? How about giving someone else that pick-me-up? Tell someone something worth remembering.

Without conviction, there is no passion.
Without passion, there is no drive.
Without drive -
there is no better tomorrow.